Park

Capstone Short Biographies

African-American Inventors

Lonnie Johnson, Frederick McKinley Jones,
Marjorie Stewart Joyner, Elijah McCoy,
Garrett Augustus Morgan

by Fred M.B. Amram

C A P S T O N E   P R E S S

MANKATO

C A P S T O N E   P R E S S
818 North Willow Street • Mankato, MN 56001

Printed in the United States of America.

Library of Congress Cataloging-in-Publication Data
Amram, Fred M.B.
  African-American inventors / Fred M.B. Amram
  p. cm.
  Includes bibliographical references and index.
  Summary: Brief biographical profiles of five African-American inventors.
  ISBN 1-56065-361-2
  1. Afro-American inventors--Biography--Juvenile literature.
[1. Inventors. 2. Afro-Americans--Biography.] I. Title.
T39.A55 1996
609.2'273--dc20

95-47863
CIP
AC r96

Photo credits
Sandra A. Brick: 4
Thermo King, Minneapolis: 6, 14, 18
Courtesy of Lonnie Johnson: 8
U.S. Patent Office: 11, 12, 16, 22, 30, 37, 41, 42, 44
Chicago Daily Defender: 20
Library of Congress: 25
Moorland-Spingarn Research Center, Howard University: 28
The Western Reserve Historical Society, Cleveland, Ohio: 34, 38

Table of Contents

Words in **boldface** type in the text are defined
in the Glossary in the back of this book.

Chapter 1

What Is an Inventor?

Y ou may not know it, but you are an inventor. More than once, you have probably invented new rules to a game. When someone makes you happy, you invent a way to say thank you. When you daydream, you are inventing stories.

Inventions can take many forms, and they can affect our lives in many different ways. The law that controls traffic on streets by telling us that we can drive no more than 30 miles per hour is an invention. The garbage truck that collects and grinds garbage is an invention, too. These inventions have changed the way we live. Imagine what a big city would be like without traffic laws, or without machinery for collecting garbage.

Marjorie Stewart Joyner invented Joyner's Permanent Waving Machine in 1928.

Frederick McKinley Jones invented refrigerated trucks.

In this book, you will meet several inventors. Some made big changes. Some made small changes. But each of these inventors is important, because their inventions have changed our lives. How would life be different if the traffic light and the gas mask had not been invented? Garrett Morgan changed our lives with these important inventions.

Without Frederick Jones we would not have ice cream trucks that roam the streets. More importantly, we would not have refrigerated trucks that bring food from farm to market.

Patent Protection

Many inventors protect their ideas with **patents**. They send their ideas to the United States Patent and Trademark Office. A patent examiner checks to see if the idea is really new and useful. If the patent examiner agrees that a patent should be granted, the ideas, often with drawings, are printed in a book. Then everyone in the world may look at the idea, can build on the idea, but cannot profit from the idea for 17 years. The idea is public, and yet the inventor is protected from theft.

After you have finished reading about the inventors in this book, you can look around for objects that need improving or problems that need solving. Find a better way. Invent solutions. Perhaps one day you will own patents for new ideas. Perhaps you will be a famous inventor.

Chapter 2

Lonnie Johnson
1949-

Aneka Johnson was one lucky kid. Her dad gave her the first Super Soaker ever built. He invented it.

Aneka's dad was working on one of his many other inventions, a CFC-free **heat pump** that would not harm the environment. Suddenly a nozzle shot out a powerful stream of water. Instead of fixing the leak, Lonnie Johnson saw an opportunity.

Lonnie Johnson invented the Super Soaker. He gave the first one he ever built to his daughter, Aneka.

Johnson figured out what made the jet stream occur. Then he applied this knowledge to the idea of a water pistol. From the idea he built a test model. Inventors call the test model a prototype. Johnson gave the model to his daughter.

Aneka became the envy of the kids in her neighborhood. Her dad realized that if he perfected the water pistol, he could have it manufactured and sold. He might make a profit.

Since Aneka's first model, more than $200 million worth of Super Soakers have been sold. Some of that money went toward manufacturing the product. Some was used for advertising and selling. Some of the profit went to Lonnie Johnson.

To protect his ideas, Johnson has more than 20 patents for his different inventions. In 1986, he received a patent for a new squirt gun. Johnson keeps improving on his product, and he has received several patents for improvements on his water pistol.

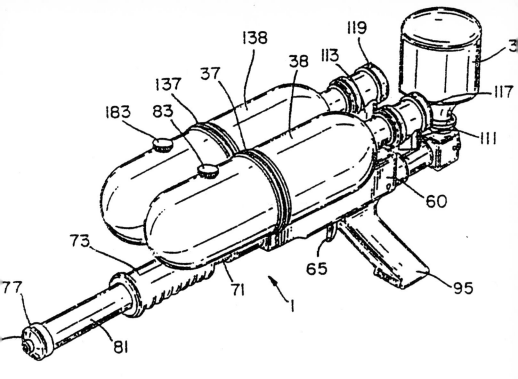

Lonnie Johnson received a patent for a new squirt gun called a Super Soaker in 1986.

Some inventors make and sell their own products. Other inventors sell their ideas and let others worry about manufacturing and **marketing**. Johnson decided to license his Super Soaker. That means he came to an agreement with a company to make and sell his product. In return, Johnson receives a certain amount of money for each Soaker the company sells.

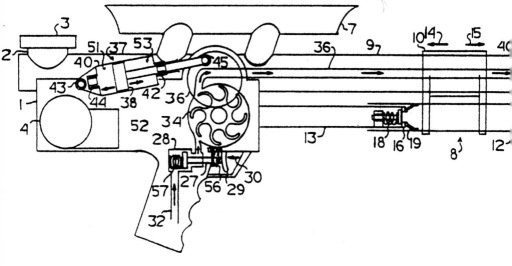

Drawings and a description of the Super Soaker are kept at the U.S. Patent Office.

Johnson loved inventing even when he was young. His mother supported him and encouraged him to study and read. She said, "It's what you put in your head that counts. Nobody can take that away from you." At 18, Johnson won a contest for inventing a robot.

After high school, Johnson earned a bachelor of science degree in mechanical engineering. Later he finished a **master of science** degree in nuclear engineering at

Tuskegee University. While in the U.S. Air Force, he became a captain and worked on space systems such as Voyager and Galileo.

Johnson keeps inventing, and he now has patents for such devices as a smoke-detecting device, an automatic sprinkler control, a wet diaper detector, and a hair curler drying apparatus.

Keeps Improving

What happened to that leaky heat pump that caused Johnson to think of his water pistol? He keeps making improvements on that invention. **NASA** is interested in using this invention because it is environmentally friendly and more efficient than traditional heat pumps and air conditioners.

Vernon Brabham Jr. is well-known for helping inventors become successful. In an interview with Lonnie Johnson printed in a magazine called *Inventor's Digest*, Brabham asked what advice Johnson would give inventors. Johnson said, **"Perseverance**! There is no short easy route to success. . . It takes a lot of hard work and a bit of luck to be successful."

Chapter 3

Frederick McKinley Jones
1893-1961

When the ice cream truck comes to your neighborhood, you can thank a man named Frederick Jones. He invented refrigerated trucks.

Ice cream is not the only food delivered by trucks. Before Jones' invention, many kinds of food often spoiled before reaching grocery stores. Farmers lost money. Consumers became sick. Jones solved that problem and changed an industry.

Born in 1893, Frederick Jones was an orphan during most of his boyhood. He did not go to school past the eighth grade, but he loved to work

Frederick Jones held many patents for things he invented.

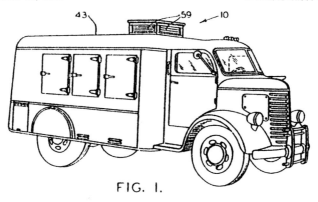

FIG. I.

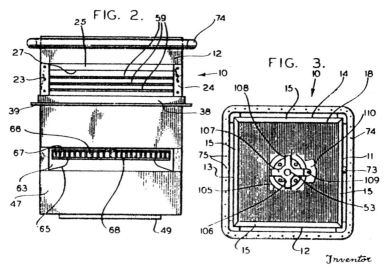

FIG. 2.

FIG. 3.

Inventor

FREDERICK M. JONES

By P. A. Whiteley

Attorney

with mechanical devices. As a teenager, he worked as an automobile mechanic and built race cars. During military service in World War I (1914-1918), he studied electricity and electronics.

After his military service, Jones drifted from job to job and city to city. He ended up in Hallock, a small town in Minnesota, where he was first employed as a farm machinery mechanic.

First Patent

As a farm mechanic, Jones learned that food was brought to market in trucks loaded with ice. Sometimes the ice melted before the trucks reached the market. When he heard about a whole shipment of **poultry** that spoiled because the truck's ice melted, he decided to invent an air conditioner for trucks. In 1949, Jones received the first of his 40 patents for portable air cooling units.

That invention changed the trucking industry and the way we shop for food. Food now arrives at the market fresher than in the past, so people do not need to shop as often. Food can also be shipped long distances without spoiling.

Eventually, Jones became an important expert in

Frederick Jones' invention changed the way we shop.

Frederick Jones was an expert in refrigeration.

refrigeration. Engineers came to him for advice and training. After World War II (1939-1945), Jones became a consultant to many agencies including the United States government.

Jones' creativity did not stop with portable refrigeration. He held 20 additional patents for inventions such as a portable X-ray machine, movie sound equipment, a self-starting gasoline engine, and other devices for controlling temperature.

Offers Advice

Jones had this advice for young people wanting to succeed:

1. Do not be afraid to get your hands dirty.

2. Read. Find out what others know. Use libraries.

3. Believe in yourself.

Tonight at dinner, imagine how food used to be delivered and think about how Frederick Jones changed all that. Think of the man who received 60 patents to attest to a true creative genius.

Think of the man who made the ice cream truck possible.

Chapter 4

Marjorie Stewart Joyner
1896-1994

Marjorie Stewart Joyner started her career as a beautician. She moved on to become an inventor and business executive, finally dedicating her life to racial and gender equality in Chicago's black community and throughout the United States.

Marjorie Stewart was born in the South, the granddaughter of a slave. Stewart moved to Chicago to live with her divorced mother who had moved north to become a maid. There Stewart married Robert Joyner who became a doctor of **podiatry**.

Marjorie Stewart Joyner was vice president of a national chain of 200 beauty colleges.

21

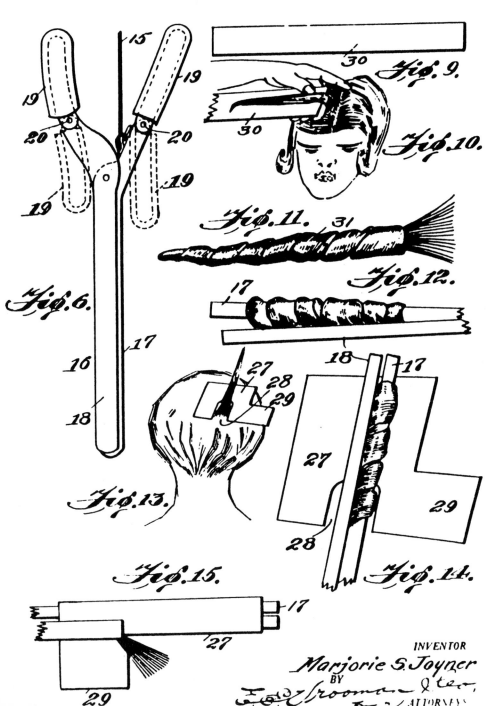

INVENTOR

Marjorie S. Joyner

BY

Fred Grooman *ter,*

ATTORNEYS

Early in her career, Joyner worked in a beauty parlor where she was trained to style white women's hair. After she married Robert, she tried to impress her new mother-in-law by providing her with free hair care.

Walker School

The elder Mrs. Joyner was not impressed, however, pointing out that Marjorie knew nothing about styling the hair of African Americans. Her mother-in-law recommended that Marjorie study at one of the Walker schools, a chain that had been developed by Madame C.J. Walker. Walker had made a fortune by developing hair and skin products for African American women. She also began a chain of hair salons and beauty schools.

Joyner learned quickly that tight, kinky hair needed special treatment. At the time, many black women preferred to have their hair curled. That meant removing the kinks with various types of straighteners.

In 1929, Marjorie Stewart Joyner patented a scalp protector that made the curling process more comfortable.

The process for curling or waving hair usually meant heating a curling iron that looked very much like a pair of dull scissors. At first, the irons were heated in or on a stove. After electricity became available, the irons were heated internally. Still, curling hair was a slow, uncomfortable process. Curls had to be set one at a time. A **hank** of hair was placed in the scissors' grip. Then the hair was twirled around the iron and held for a while.

More Efficient

Joyner thought that the curling process would be more efficient if a group of curling irons could be hung above a woman's head. Each clip could capture a hank of hair, and the machine could be plugged into an electric outlet. That way, an entire head of curls or waves could be set at once.

Joyner's invention was called the Permanent Waving Machine. After the 1928 patent was assigned to the Madame C.J. Walker Manufacturing Company, the device was used

Interior View
Madame C. J. Walker's Hair Parlors

Marjorie Stewart Joyner's patents were assigned to Madame C.J. Walker's company.

in the entire chain of Walker beauty salons and schools.

The waving machine also found an unexpected market. While black women often wanted to change their hair's kink to a curl, many white women wanted to add curl to their straighter hair. Soon beauticians serving the much larger white market wanted the Joyner Permanent Wave Machine.

Although her invention was a success, Joyner wanted to improve it. Even with the new Permanent Wave Machine, the curling process was uncomfortable for the person whose hair was being waved. The irons were hot and pinched the scalp. Joyner invented a Scalp Protector to make the curling process more comfortable. This 1929 patent was also assigned to the Walker Company.

Joyner was later selected for the board of directors of the Walker Company. She had a knack for business, and she went on to become vice president of a national chain of 200 Walker beauty colleges.

In the 1940s, Joyner founded the United Beauty School Owners and Teachers Association. After achieving success as an inventor and entrepreneur, Joyner decided to return to school to earn her own **doctorate** degree. Eventually, she earned a Ph.D. in the humanities.

In 1987, Joyner's work was featured as part of a Smithsonian exhibition. She was remembered for her public service, including membership on President Franklin Roosevelt's campaign committee. Joyner worked with Mary McCleod Bethune and Eleanor Roosevelt on issues that concerned women and the African American community.

Contributions to Beauty

But most of all we remember her for her contributions to beauty. Clients at her beauty shop included Billie Holiday, Lena Horne, Ethel Waters, Marian Anderson, and Louis Armstrong. Joyner contributed many of her business profits to African American societies that served children and the arts.

Joyner died just after Christmas in 1994, at the age of 98. On hearing of Joyner's death, Illinois Senator Carol Moseley Braun said, "Dr. Joyner proved that excellence and discipline and commitment will win out in the long run."

Chapter 5

Elijah McCoy

1844-1929

Elijah McCoy was a true genius, the inventor of 50 patented ideas. Most of all, McCoy's name stood for quality. Even now when people want top quality, they say "I want the real McCoy."

McCoy lived at a time when railroads were changing the nation. Tracks were laid from east to west and from north to south. The North American West was built by the railroads, which made transporting people and goods possible.

McCoy was born in Canada, into a community of escaped slaves. As a young man, he went to

Elijah McCoy invented an automatic lubricator for engines.

E. McCOY.

LUBRICATOR.

No. 255,443.　　　　　　　　　　Patented Mar. 28, 18

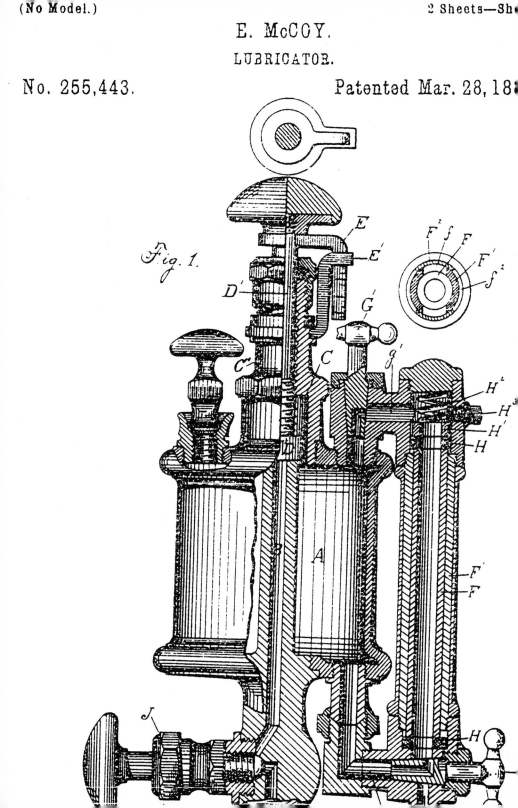

Fig. 1.

Scotland to **apprentice** as a mechanical engineer. When he returned to North America, he ended up in Michigan, at the home of the Michigan Central Railroad.

Puts Skills to Use

Although he was trained as an engineer, the best job he could get was as a stoker, the worker who kept the fire burning on steam-powered locomotives. McCoy soon put his engineering skills to use to resolve a common problem faced by the railroad.

Locomotive engines have many moving parts that rub against each other. If you rub your hands together quickly and for a long time they will become hot. In the same way, a steam engine's parts overheated when they rubbed together too long. The heat could cause damage to the engine parts and could even start fires.

Elijah McCoy kept inventing until he died in 1929.

The only way to prevent overheating was to frequently oil, or lubricate, the engine's parts.

As a stoker for the Michigan Central Railroad, part of McCoy's job was to lubricate the engine by hand. The train had to be stopped each time he oiled the engine's parts. The stops caused great delays in the train's schedules, and even with careful oiling, engine parts overheated often. Then the parts had to be repaired or replaced, causing even greater delays.

McCoy knew there had to be a better way to lubricate the engines. He applied his engineering training to this important problem.

Invents Lubricator

First, in 1872, McCoy invented a lubricator that did not require a worker to do the job by hand. The train had to stand still while the lubricator was in use, but this method was safer and worked better and faster than the old method. The railroad was pleased with

McCoy's work and encouraged him to improve his invention. Ten years later, McCoy patented a lubricator that worked while a train or ship was moving. The lubricator automatically dripped oil on moving parts as needed.

The Real McCoy

McCoy invented many versions of the lubricator. Some were used with engines in motion. Others were used with engines standing still in factories. The automatic lubricator was so popular that other engineers started to design their own versions. However, none were as good. When customers bought a lubricator they asked, "Is this the real McCoy?"

McCoy did not stay with the railroad. He became a teacher, instructing others about the use of his lubricator and about other workings of engines. And he never stopped inventing.

Chapter 6

Garrett Augustus Morgan

1877-1963

The next time you cross the street at a traffic light, you can thank Garrett Morgan for his invention that tells cars to stop and go.

Every time firefighters enter a smoky building, they wear gas masks that permit them to breathe. They may not know that Garrett Morgan invented these safety hoods. They may not know that he became a hero when he first demonstrated their use. But they are thankful to have the product of Morgan's work.

Morgan was born in 1877, 12 years after the Civil War (1861-1865) ended. By the time he

In 1923, Garrett Morgan patented his automatic traffic signal.

was 35 years old, Morgan had a successful business manufacturing beauty products in Cleveland, Ohio. He had enough money to take a break from his business to think about a new problem that concerned him. He was interested in workers' safety.

In 1914, Morgan patented a safety hood or breathing device, an early version of the gas mask. He designed it for workers whose jobs exposed them to poisonous fumes. Unfortunately, people were not convinced that Morgan's hood was useful.

Tragedy Strikes

In 1916, a tragedy became an opportunity for Morgan. An explosion ripped through a tunnel under Lake Erie. The tunnel was being built to create a shortcut for traveling. Police and firefighters failed in attempts to rescue workers trapped in the tunnel. Several firefighters died. Morgan rushed to the scene. Wearing his gas mask, he entered the tunnel again and again. Each time, he carried out another worker who had been

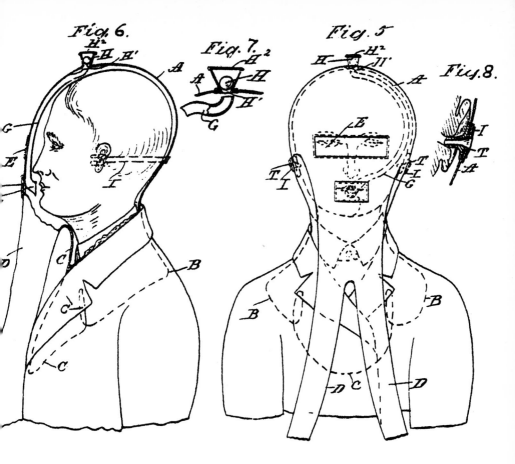

Garrett Morgan's safety hood protected workers whose jobs exposed them to poisonous fumes.

overcome by the poisonous air. Several assistants placed safety hoods on their heads and helped Morgan with the rescue work. Some of the tunnel workers had already died, but others were alive.

An explosion in 1916 proved that Garrett Morgan's safety hood worked. Morgan became a hero.

Garrett Morgan's heroism became big news, and newspapers praised his wonderful invention. Orders for his breathing device poured in from fire departments all across the United States.

Unfortunately, prejudice nearly got in the way of Morgan's success. Some people canceled orders when they found out that the inventor of the safety hood was black. On some sales trips, Morgan hired a white man to impersonate him.

Not Discouraged

Garrett Morgan was not discouraged by other people's prejudice. He continued to think of ways to make the world a safer place.

By 1920, American streets became crowded with automobiles competing with horse-drawn wagons. Accidents were quite common. In big cities, pedestrians were afraid to cross streets.

Police officers helped to control traffic. Sometimes they carried big signs that told drivers when to stop and when to go. It was a simple but often unsuccessful solution to traffic problems. Accidents still happened.

Garrett Morgan saw a need for a new traffic signal. He designed a signal that consisted of a tall post with movable arms. A traffic monitor or police officer turned a crank to make the post rotate and to make the arms go up and down.

In the open position, the arms stretched out telling drivers to stop. At the end of each arm, facing the cross traffic, was the word "go." When the monitor turned the crank, the arms were raised. Now the traffic lanes that had been looking at the tips of the arms, which told them to go, saw the underside of the arms instead, which told these drivers to stop.

When the crank was turned further, the whole post rotated a quarter turn and the arms opened up again. Now drivers on the other street saw the word "go" on the tip of the arms. After a while, the monitor turned the crank and the whole process repeated.

Creative Features

Two features of Morgan's traffic signal were especially creative. First, several lights were installed in the post so that the words "stop" and "go" could be lighted up at night. Sometimes the posts used batteries to power the lights.

G. A. MORGAN.

BREATHING DEVICE.

APPLICATION FILED AUG. 19, 1912.

1,113,675.

Patented Oct. 13, 1914.

2 SHEETS—SHEET 1.

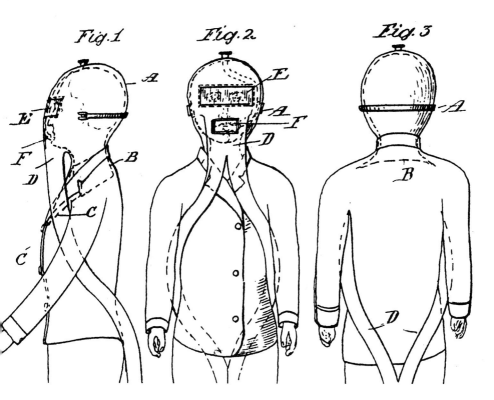

Fig. 1   Fig. 2   Fig. 3

Some people canceled their orders for Garrett Morgan's safety hood when they found out the inventor was black.

Sometimes the posts used electricity, which was just becoming available in big cities. The electricity to power the signal came from overhead wires that also powered trolley cars, a kind of electric bus that ran on tracks.

Nov. 20, 1923.

G. A. MORGAN

1,475,024

TRAFFIC SIGNAL

Filed Feb. 27, 1922

2 Sheets-Sheet 1

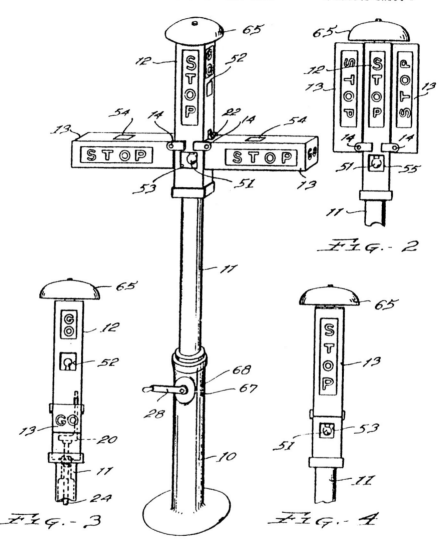

FIG.-2

FIG.-3

FIG.-1

FIG.-4

INVENTOR
Garrett A. Morgan,
By Bates & Macklin,
ATTORNEYS

A second special feature of Morgan's traffic signal was a set of bells that rang when the post was changing direction. While the crank was turning, bells alerted drivers and pedestrians to the change that was about to take place. Some modern traffic signals still use Garrett Morgan's attention-getting bells.

Immediate Success

In 1923, Morgan patented his automatic traffic signal. It was an immediate success. Eager to return to business, he started the G.A. Morgan Safety System Company. Eventually he sold the rights to his traffic signal patent to the General Electric Company.

Traffic signals have come a long way since 1923, but the changes were based on Garrett Morgan's ideas. Inventors often make changes to existing products when they see a need for improvement, and when they find a better way.

Garrett Morgan's traffic signal was a tall post with movable arms. The arms told drivers when to stop and go.

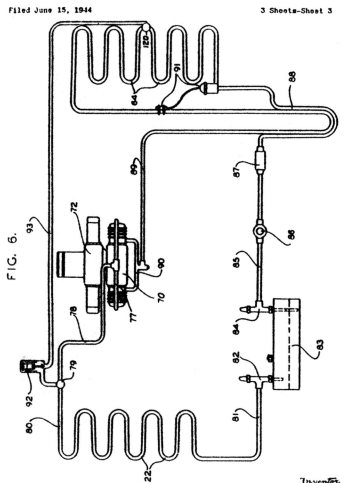

FIG. 6.

Inventor

FREDERICK M. JONES

By [signature]

Attorney

Glossary

apprentice—work for low pay or without pay to learn a trade

doctorate—the highest degree awarded by a university

hank—a loop or coil of something

heat pump—a device that uses outdoor air to heat or cool enclosed areas

marketing—packaging, advertising, and selling goods to the consumer

master of science degree—a college or university degree awarded after graduate study

NASA—National Aeronautics and Space Administration

patent—an official document that grants exclusive rights for a specific time

perseverance—the quality that allows a person to continue to try despite difficulties

podiatry—study and treatment of foot ailments

poultry—birds raised for meat and eggs, such as chickens, turkeys, and ducks

The best inventions make our lives better.

To Learn More

Haskins, James. *Outward Dreams: Black Inventors and Their Inventions.* New York: Walker, 1991.

McDonald, Anne L. *Feminine Ingenuity: Women and Invention in America.* New York: Ballantine, 1992.

McKissack, Pat. *African-American Inventors.* Brookfield, Conn.: Millbrook Press, 1994.

Showell, Ellen H. and Fred M.B. Amram. *From Indian Corn to Outer Space: Women Invent in America.* Peterborough, N.H.: Cobblestone Publishing, 1995.

Towle, Wendy. *The Real McCoy: The Life of an African-American Inventor.* New York: Scholastic, 1989.

Useful Addresses

International Inventors Assistance League
345 West Cypress Street
Glendale, CA 91204

Inventors Clubs of America
P.O. Box 450261
Atlanta, GA 31145-0261

**Inventors Workshop International
  Education Foundation**
7332 Mason Avenue
Canoga Park, CA 91306

National Inventive Thinking Association
P.O. Box 836202
Richardson, TX 75083

Women Inventors Project
1 Greensboro Drive, Suite 302
Etobicoke, ON M9W 1C8
Canada

Index